Body Numbers

Contents

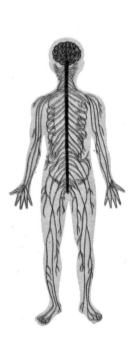

Rigby

Body Numbers

Two eyes, **ten** fingers, **twenty** baby teeth. These are some body numbers that you know, but there are many more.

2 eyes

2 hands

2 ears

2 legs

10 toes

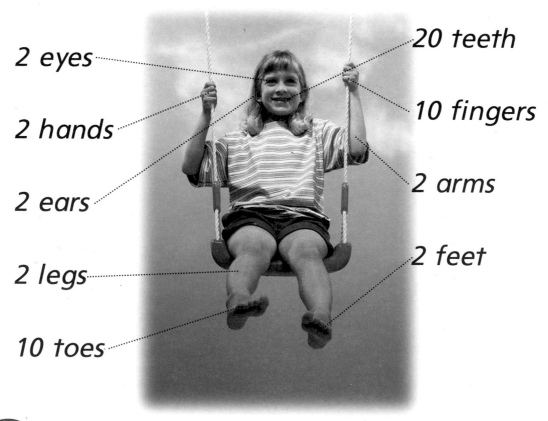

20 teeth

10 fingers

2 arms

2 feet

Cells

Your body is made up of **trillions** of tiny cells! There are many different kinds of cells.

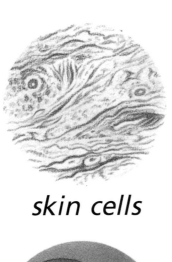
skin cells

muscle cells

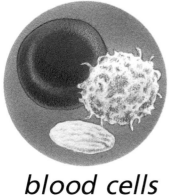
blood cells

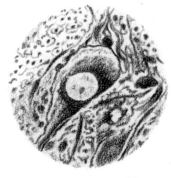
nerve cells

Bones

You have about **206** bones in your body. Together, they form your skeleton.

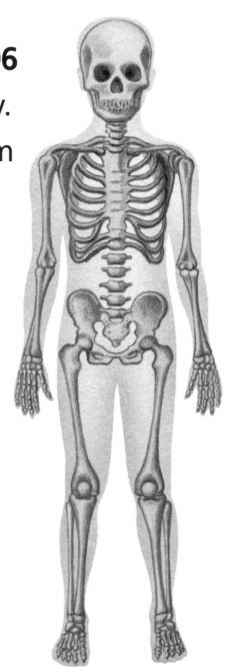

Do you know which part of your skeleton has the most bones in it? Your hand does! Each one of your hands has **27** bones.

27 + 27 = 54 bones

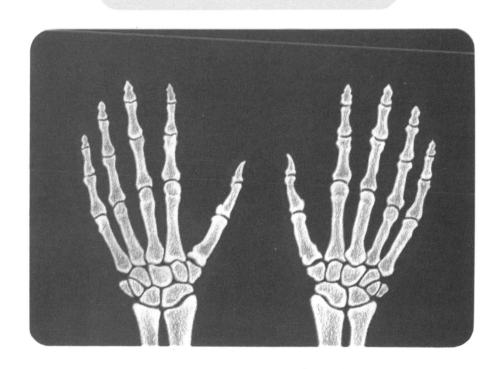

Muscles

Your body has more than **600** muscles. They help you move, hold a pencil, and chew food. They also help you blink and smile.

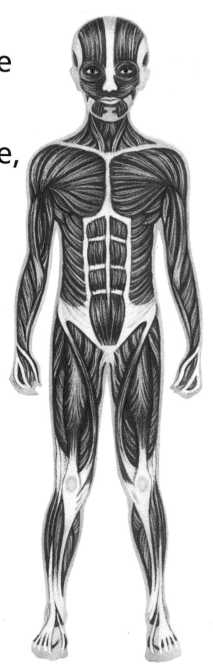

Your muscles make up about half the weight of your body. This means if you weigh **50** pounds, you have about **25** pounds of muscle.

other
muscle things

Heart

Your heart has **four** chambers. The chambers pump blood around your body. The beating of your heart is the sound of the chambers working.

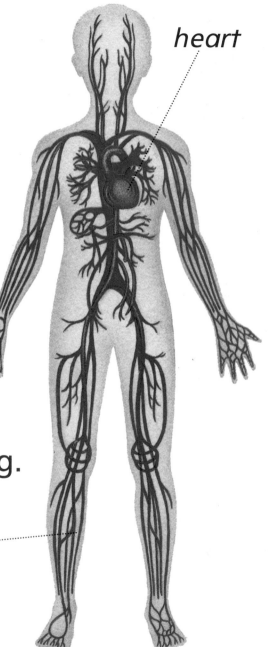

heart

blood vessels

When you sit still, your heart beats about **60** to **80** times per minute. When you exercise, it can beat up to **200** times per minute.

*Sitting still =
60 to 80 beats
per minute*

*Exercising =
100 to 200 beats
per minute*

Brain

Your brain gets messages from every part of your body. It sends messages back to your body through **billions** of nerve cells.

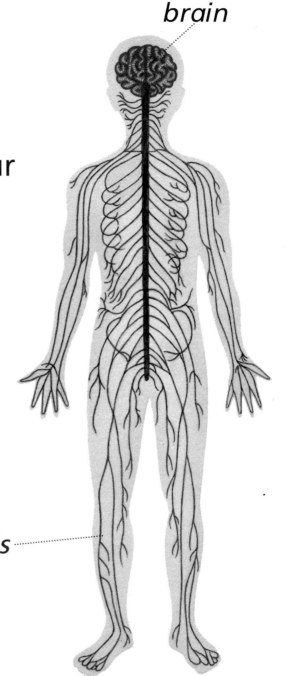

brain

nerve cells

When messages are very important, your brain can send them faster than **200** miles per hour!

When the water is too hot, your brain quickly sends a message to move your hands.

Senses

Your body has **five** senses. They are sight, hearing, smell, taste, and touch.

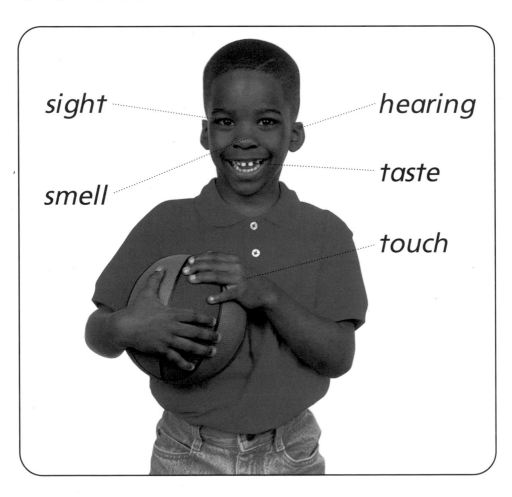

sight

hearing

taste

smell

touch

Do you know which **three** senses help you enjoy food? Sight, smell, and taste do. If you could not see or smell your food, it would not taste as good.

smell   taste   sight

Amazing Body

Every day, your body grows about **2 billion** new cells!

You blink your eyes about **20,000** times a day!

When you smile, you use about **15** muscles.

Your tongue has about **10,000** tiny taste buds. They can taste sweet, sour, salty, and bitter foods.

Most people's noses can smell about **4,000** different smells. Really sensitive noses can smell up to **10,000** smells!

Index